Blake Griffin: The Inspiring Story of One of Basketball's Most Dominant Power Forwards

An Unauthorized Biography

By: Clayton Geoffreys

Table of Contents

Foreword...1

Introduction 3

Chapter 1: Childhood and Early Life 7

Chapter 2: High School Years 14

Chapter 3: College Years at Oklahoma 20

Chapter 4: Blake's NBA Career 36

Chapter 5: Griffin's Personal Life 82

Chapter 6: Impact on Basketball 90

Chapter 7: Blake Griffin's Legacy and Future 95

Final Word/About the Author.......................................99

Foreword

Few big men in the NBA today entertain crowds as much as Blake Griffin. His dynamic dunks and high-energy style of play drives the fans wild. It's no surprise why the Los Angeles Clippers have quickly become one of the most entertaining teams to watch in the recent NBA seasons. Year after year, Blake Griffin has defied critics, by building upon his game, which once was labeled as "one-dimensional." Now growing increasingly confident with his outside shot, Griffin has and will continue to develop into a truly all-around dominant big man in the league. Alongside the leadership of Chris Paul at the point guard position, the Clippers have turned their franchise's fortunes around with several consecutive playoff appearances. Blake Griffin's selection as the number one overall pick started it all. Thank you for purchasing *Blake Griffin: The Inspiring Story of One of Basketball's Most Dominant Power Forwards*. In this unauthorized biography, we will learn Blake Griffin's incredible life story and impact on the game of basketball. Hope you enjoy and if you do, please do not forget to leave a review! Also, check out my website at claytongeoffreys.com to join my exclusive list where I let you know about my latest books and give you goodies!

Cheers,

Clayton Geoffreys

Visit me at www.claytongeoffreys.com

Introduction

If you regularly watch ESPN SportsCenter's daily top 10 plays, then there's a good chance that you have seen Los Angeles Clippers' power forward, Blake Griffin many times. In the span of his young and promising career, his flurry of electrifying, death defying, and posterizing dunks have elevated him to fame. He stands at a height of 6 feet and 10 inches and weighs 250 pounds. This stature, combined with his out-of-this-world athleticism and leaping ability, Griffin is an impressive physical specimen. Along with his running mates, such as NBA All-Star point guard Chris Paul, and fellow dunking dervish, DeAndre Jordan, Griffin is at the center of the moniker he himself coined for the team, "Lob City". His humiliation efforts against fellow big men Timofey Mozgov, Kendrick Perkins, and Pau Gasol have generated almost six million *YouTube* views. He won the NBA Slam Dunk Contest in 2011 by leaping over a car and then slamming the ball down while being serenaded by a choir singing R. Kelly's "I Believe I Can Fly". He has also been featured in numerous commercials and advertisements for brands, such as Kia (who sponsors the slam dunk contest) and Subway.

However, his best ability was also the source of his greatest criticism. Many basketball experts, including hall-of-fame power forward, Charles Barkley; have dismissed Griffin as a one-dimensional dunker. They claimed that he doesn't have a refined post-up game, relies too much on his physical gifts, and has limited basketball acumen. His poor free-throw shooting and playoff struggles haven't helped his case either.

Even contemporaries dislike his tough guy on-court persona, the way he looks at his opponents with a stone-cold expression after his dunks, and his constant flopping. Zach Randolph of the Memphis Grizzlies called Griffin an "actor" prior to their 2012 playoff matchup.

However, for Blake, this isn't the first time in his life that he has had to overcome adversity. He wasn't even the best Griffin at basketball in the family once. His older brother, Taylor, who had an eight-game stint with the Phoenix Suns back in 2009, used to always beat him when they played in their driveway when they were young. He also had to work his way back and prove that he was worthy of being selected number one overall in the 2009 NBA Draft after a knee injury robbed him of his rookie season.

Now, entering his fifth season, with arguably the best point guard in the league throwing him alley-oops, a championship-winning coach, and a reliable mix of veteran teammates, Blake Griffin has everything he needs in his road to stardom. Currently, he is just scratching the surface of a potentially long and rewarding NBA career. Part of his success could be credited to his family being involved with the sport since he and his older brother were youngsters playing at home before being home-schooled until they were both in high school. Another factor was his work ethic from high school, college and all the way up to the NBA. All these factors led to his development to become one of the most popular players in the NBA today.

Chapter 1: Childhood and Early Life

Blake Austin Griffin was born on March 16, 1989 in Oklahoma City, Oklahoma. His father, Tommy, was of Afro-Haitian descent and a former high school basketball and track star. He owned a trophy company and was Blake's high school coach. His mother, Gail, a Caucasian, was a former high school teacher. Their marriage was one of the few interracial relations at that time. Both his parents taught their sons, Blake and his older brother Taylor, who was three years Blake's senior, that the pillars of success were hard work and discipline.

Tommy Griffin was an athlete in his own right while going to school at Northwestern Oklahoma State University – a Division II program in the National Collegiate Athletic Association's Great American Conference – where he was inducted into the school's sports Hall of Fame on January 13, 2006. While studying there from 1966-1970, Tommy Griffin was a two-sport athlete. He averaged a double-double in all four years with the Rangers while also competing in several events in track and field, which included pole vault, high jump, discus throw, and the javelin. After graduation, he would begin his coaching career at Classen High School and won a few state championships before moving to a couple of different schools in Oklahoma. Overall, after about 29 years as a head coach, he had a total of six state championships in basketball with a combined record of 456-203. This was the man who taught the game to young Blake and Taylor, who were practicing their lessons against each other in one-on-one contests well before they would become teammates in high school and college.

In the meantime, the Griffin boys' mother, Gail, home-schooled both her sons until Blake and Taylor were in the equivalent of eighth grade and sophomore year in high school, respectively. The brothers grew up in an environment where they had a long list of chores, curfew and church. His father explained their decision to "deviate from the norm" and gave his sons a foundation where God is in the center of their lives. Blake was a mother's boy. He loved her mother's strawberry cake. His mother always encouraged her son's penchant for creativity, which might be the reason for the artistic nature of Blake's highlight-reel-worthy dunks.

Growing up, the Griffin brothers may have been bereft of schoolmates, but they had plenty of teammates and rivals growing up, including each other. Both of them were both gifted athletes competing in youth leagues for different sports, such as baseball, football, and, of course, basketball. They had numerous driveway battles, which Taylor won almost every time. It was for this reason that Blake was called "Little Griffin" by everyone they knew, much to his annoyance. However, Blake's losses would eventually lead him to toughen up. Eventually, Little Griffin's youthful exuberance led him to turn every little thing into a competition between him and his elder brother.

However, the competitiveness the Griffin brothers have towards each other has also led to the unbreakable bond they share up to this day.

One of Blake's closest childhood friends is the Philadelphia Eagles' current quarterback, Sam Bradford, in the National Football League, who was also a first overall selection by the St. Louis Rams in the 2011 NFL Draft. Blake himself was the first overall selection in the 2009 NBA Draft. The two friends attended Oklahoma University, where Bradford had some success in college as the Sooners' quarterback where he would have a career of 8,403 passing yards, 88 touchdowns, and 16 interceptions. Before that, he was growing up with others playing sports at the family's sports complex.

Bradford's parents owned a gym in Edmonds, Oklahoma and they would get all their trophies from Tommy Griffin, whose company made them. As a result, Blake and Taylor would get to play ball a lot with Sam in their complex. The young Bradford was an only child who was spending a lot of time playing sports of many kinds – football, basketball, baseball, hockey, and golf. Bradford was also playing a lot of AAU basketball while in high school with Blake – but that shall be discussed at another section.

Growing up, Blake Griffin played many sports other than basketball and the Bradford-owned gym was a good way to remain active. The soon-to-be basketball star also played a lot of baseball in his youth, mostly as a first baseman. He admitted later on in life that baseball was his second favorite choice because he could "go without hitting for a month and still have fun."

Before deciding to ultimately focus on basketball, Blake also played a little bit of football in his childhood and played in different positions. He played as a wide receiver, tight end and safety, positions that would be fitting of someone above the six-foot mark in height in those years. In addition to that, both Blake and his brother played some soccer, but neither had gained a lot of success on the sport like they did in basketball.

Blake would later tell reporters that his parents wanted them to try a little bit of everything. Thus, in addition to basketball, they tried soccer, track and field, and even swimming. The goal of their parents was to be open and allow their children to play any sport they had an interest in because there was something to learn from just about any sport. In a video interview with the Los Angeles Times, Blake said his father wanted him to play soccer to gain the footwork skills that were beneficial in other sports like basketball, and that, "Everything you play helps in what you select in the end," Blake said.

Eventually, Blake's parents allowed him to choose which sport he would focus on, and although baseball was one of his favorites, he chose basketball. While some people believed that Blake could have found success if he continued playing football, Blake was certain that he was meant for the basketball court, a sport which he was greatly passionate about. As it turned out, there were a lot of people in Los Angeles who were glad he made that decision early on.

Chapter 2: High School Years

After years of having their home as their classroom, the Griffin brothers finally came out of homeschooling and enrolled in Oklahoma Christian School in 2003 when Blake was entering his freshman year and older brother Taylor entered his junior year. The school was located in Edmond, Oklahoma – a wealthy suburb north of Oklahoma City. Their home life still followed them as their father Tommy was the coach for the Saints' basketball team.

After years of competing against each other in the driveway, the brothers relished the opportunity to finally be on the same side. They led the Saints to back-to-back state championships in 2004 and 2005. In Blake's freshman year, the Saints finished with a perfect 29-0 record en route to capturing the Class 3A Boys' Championship and won against Riverside Indian School, 55-50. However, the team, nor Blake, would settle for just one championship.

The Saints repeated their champion performance in Blake's sophomore year. He scored 12 points and grabbed 9 rebounds in their 51-34 victory against Sequoyah-Tahlequah in the 3A Championship game on March 12, 2005. The elder Taylor grabbed all the headlines for his stellar play and bagging the Oklahoma's Player of the Year honors that season, which was his last for the Saints. Both brothers were named to the Little All-City All-State team, and despite the praises Taylor was getting, Blake was starting to make a name for himself.

During the summer of 2005, Blake played in the Athletes First AAU team along with childhood friend Sam Bradford and Xavier Henry, a future NBA colleague. On July 24, 2005, he first he encountered current NBA players Kevin Durant and Ty Lawson, who were both members of the DC Blue Devils' AAU squad. While Durant led all players on the court with 29 points, Blake was able to hold his own with 15 points in that game that featured plenty of athletic talent despite his team losing the summer exhibition.

Taylor went on to college at the University of Oklahoma Sooners, and Blake became the team's unquestioned leader in his junior season. He began to catch the attention of college scouts as his game began to blossom. His strength and athleticism were translating to more matured performances on the court. He led the Saints to the championship for the third consecutive year scoring 22 points, amassing 9 rebounds, and blocking 6 shots in their 57-40 conquest of Washington High School on March 11, 2006. In his junior season, Blake averaged 21.7 points, 12.5 rebounds, and 4.9 assists and was named the State Tournament MVP.

He was also recognized as the Oklahoman Player of the Year and made the Tulsa World Boys All-State First Team. His brother's college coach, Jeff Capel, also started to notice him. He was impressed by

Blake's combination of size, strength, and athleticism. He was convinced that Blake was the player he needed to rebuild Oklahoma's basketball program. At that time Oklahoma was barred from recruiting players outside their campus for a year due to the telephone recruitment controversies that previous coach, Kelvin Sampson, got caught up in. He began to make overtures in recruiting Blake, but Blake also considered going to other college powerhouses, such as Duke, Kansas, North Carolina, and Texas. The prodding of older brother Taylor and the convenience of playing close to home, however, was enough to convince Blake to commit to Oklahoma even before his senior season started.

Blake took his game to another level in his senior year of high school, finishing with eye-popping numbers of 26.8 points, 15.1 rebounds, 4.9 assists, and 2.9 blocks, leading the Saints to the state championship for the final time with a squad that averaged nearly 68 points per game – an offensive that is extremely rare for any high school program – to lead to a final win-loss record of 24-3. Blake had a game where he finished with a monster triple-double stat line of 41 points, 28 rebounds, and 10 assists to help the Saints defeat Oklahoma City's Southeast High School, 90-77, on January 30, 2007.

On March 10, 2007, Blake played his final high school game in their 81-50 rout of Pawnee High School in the state title decider. In the championship win, he had 22 points, nine rebounds, six assists, and blocked two shots for a well-rounded performance that helped him, once again, to claim the state tournament MVP. Blake had an average of 26.6 points per game during that championship run with Oklahoma Christian to end a memorable four years of high school basketball.

During Blake's four-year run at Oklahoma Christian School, the Saints posted an astounding 106-6 win-loss record. Following his senior year, he was everyone's choice as Player of the Year. He made almost every

All-America high school list and was ranked among the top 25 players in the nation. He also won the Powerade Jam Fest slam-dunk competition at the McDonald's All-American game. He headed to Norman, about 45 minutes away, as one of Oklahoma's most highly-rated and decorated recruit in years.

Griffin was considered the country's 13th best player coming out of high school by the staff at HoopScoop. He was also ranked 20th best by college basketball recruiting experts at Scout.com and 23rd by Rivals.com. For each of those three websites, Griffin was a top-10 choice as one of the best power forwards who would be entering the 2007-2008 college basketball season as a freshman.

Chapter 3: College Years at Oklahoma

When he first arrived at Oklahoma, Blake was again known as Taylor Griffin's "little" brother, even though Taylor was not the star player in his first couple of season. Taylor's freshman year at Oklahoma included playing in 27 of the Sooners' 29 games with an average of 3.1 points per game as the team would finish 20-9 (11-5 Big 12) and lose in the first round of the NCAA National Championship tournament to the University of Wisconsin-Milwaukee, 82-74, on March 16, 2006.

Taylor's numbers doubled in his sophomore year during Oklahoma's 2006-2007 season as he finished with 6.3 points, 5.2 rebounds, and 1.8 assists per game. He appeared in all 31 games for the Sooners, which finished near the bottom of the conference standings with 16-15 (6-10 Big 12). Thus, no one really knew what to expect with both Griffin brothers in their team.

But by the time Blake's freshman year ended, everybody was comparing him to Sooner legend Wayman Tisdale. In the season opening home game on November 8, 2007, Blake led the team with 18 points and 13 rebounds in a 71-55 victory over the University of San Francisco as part of the first round of the 2K Sports College Hoops Classic. Blake would follow that up with another 15 points as part of an overall team victory over the University of Denver, 80-50, on November 9, 2007. However, the team lost in a showcase game in New York City against the third-ranked Memphis Wildcats, 63-53, on November 15, 2007, where Blake struggled with only eight points while Memphis was led by their star freshman, Derrick Rose.

That loss was quickly followed up with 16 points and 12 rebounds in a 74-42 blowout win at home on November 21, 2007. They had some ups and downs in the non-conference schedule, but one of their biggest wins was at home on December 20, 2007, against the

Gonzaga Bulldogs (who were ranked 18th at the time) 72-68. While senior Longar led the team with 16 points, Blake led all with 14 rebounds in what would be one of his strongest suits for the Sooners – rebounding. Likewise, he was able to score inside the paint with a combination of touch on his shots and the power behind his slam dunks. In the very next game, Blake would score 18 points and collect 16 rebounds to help contribute to a double-overtime win at West Virginia, 88-82, on December 29, 2007. By the end of their conference schedule, the Sooners were 12-3 and looked to be one of the stronger teams in the Big 12 Conference.

Blake was constantly racking up double-doubles and was one of the best players in the nation until he had a mediate collateral ligament (MCL) injury, which initially appeared to be a sprain. This happened on January 14, 2008 in a game against Kansas stopped him in his tracks. After about five minutes into the first half, he was going up for a rebound and landed weird and injured his left knee. His brother, Taylor, then made an effort to fill his younger brother's shoes while he was out, scoring a career-high 16 points and a season-high of 12 rebounds in the Sooners' 63-61 win over Texas Tech on January 19, 2008.

In an unexpected return after the sprained knee, Blake would return to the team for their round game against the Baylor Bears on January 26, 2008 in a 77-71 win, where he would pick up right where he left off with 17 points and 15 rebounds. He followed that with 15 points in the Sooners' 64-61 win on January 28, 2008 against the Oklahoma State Cowboys. In this game, his older brother contributed 20 points and six rebounds.

Two months after his initial knee injury, Blake tore the cartilage in his right knee in a game versus Texas A&M on March 1, 2008, where the Sooners won, 64-37. He had arthroscopic surgery and it was assumed that his season was over. Amazingly, he was back after a week and a half of rest in a matchup game, which they won over Missouri on March 8, 2008 with a score of 75-66. Blake had 14 points to support Austin Johnson's 18 points. The team would then switch to the Big 12 Conference tournament and would win their quarterfinals match in gritty fashion on March 14, 2008, with a 54-49 win over the Colorado Buffaloes – even though Blake only had 10 points in one of his biggest struggles of the season.

While Blake would score 20 points and collect 13 rebounds in the Big 12 tournament semifinals, the rest of the Sooners shot only 32.8 percent from the field in a 77-49 loss to the Texas Longhorns on March 15, 2008. However, there was no shame in losing to a team that would finish 31-7 overall and advanced to the Elite Eight of the NCAA National Championship tournament. Nevertheless, while the Longhorns represented the Big 12 in that NCAA Tournament, the Sooners would also make their presence felt as a sixth-seed.

The Sooners won their first round match on March 21, 2008, against the St. Joe's Hawks in a 72-64 victory. While Blake had 12 points and four rebounds in the game, the team was led by David Godbold's 25 points to advance to the second round, where they were unable to get the upset over the third-seeded Louisville Cardinals on March 23, 2008, with a score of 78-48. Griffin struggled to score points and only had eight points while collecting seven rebounds. While he did make four out of six field goals, there weren't a lot of opportunities against a Cardinals team that would make it to the Elite Eight that season.

While the Sooners left the NCAA Tournament a lot earlier than they wanted to, Blake finished his freshman season with the averages of 14.7 points and 9.1 rebounds while playing 28.4 minutes per game. He led the Sooners to a 23-12 record and finished in the top 10 of the Big 12 conference in scoring and rebounding.

Even big brother Taylor was impressed by Blake's freshman year display. Taylor admitted that he had seen things that his brother did that he had not seen before. It was only a matter of time before Blake's highlights become a regular viewing on *YouTube*. Scribes agreed as Blake garnered citations, such as first team all-district pick by the USBWA and NABC. He was also a part of the Big 12 All-Rookie team and the first team All-Big 12 selection by the league conference. He was also the first Sooner, since Tisdale in 1983, to be named to the All-Conference Rookie team for the Big 8 Conference.

At that time, Griffin was already being talked about as a potential NBA lottery pick even though he had faced limited top-flight opposition. Outside of conference play, Griffin didn't face a lot of big name programs except for Memphis (63-53 loss, November 15, 2007), and Gonzaga (72-68 win, December 20, 2007). He decided to return for his sophomore year in 2008 as he wanted to help Oklahoma make a run for the national championship. Furthermore, he felt that his game was not yet developed enough and he wanted to mature more physically to withstand the tough and demanding nature of the NBA.

The Sooners started on the right path in their quest for national glory as they won their first 12 games in Griffin's sophomore season. In Oklahoma's season opening win against American University on November 14, 2008, Griffin scored 24 points while having a total of 18 rebounds, 16 on defense, in the team's 83-54 victory. In the very next game, Griffin would make eight of his nine field goals (88.9 percent) for 20 points during the team's 94-53 blowout win over Mississippi Valley State on November 17, 2008, He also had 19 total rebounds (15 on defense, four on offense), and a season high of six steals.

During this stretch of a season-opening winning streak, Griffin had his first 20-20 game (points and rebounds) with 25 points and 21 rebounds against Davidson. He did better in the next game with 35 points and 21 rebounds against Gardner-Webb, which made him the first player in Big 12 history to record two consecutive games with at least 20 points and 20 rebounds. That game also included a season high of five assists for Griffin. His performances earned him three-straight Big 12 Player of the Week awards, and he would finish the season with a record-tying six citations.

The Arkansas Razorbacks were the team that dealt them their first loss on December 30, 2008, when the Razorback defeated the Sooners, 96-88. Griffin still had a good game with 21 points, making 8 of 15 field goals (53.3 percent) to go along with 13 points, four assists, three blocked shots, and one steal. Even though Oklahoma lost the game, Griffin showed that his overall game was improving not only on offense, but on defense as well.

His shooting efficiency was getting a lot better than his freshman season. In a home game against Maine on

December 10, 2008, Griffin made 11 of 13 field goals (84.6 percent) en route to scoring 22 points and 10 rebounds in a 78-52 win. Griffin set his career highs for points and rebounds with 40 and 23, respectively, in a 95-74 win against Texas Tech on February 14, 2009, becoming the only player to do so in the Big 12 conference, and just the third player in University of Oklahoma basketball program's history after Alvan Adams and Wayman Tisdale.

There was a step back one week later when Griffin suffered a concussion in the first half of the Sooners' February 21, 2009, game at Texas, where they lost 73-68. Before exiting the game early, Griffin only had two points out of five total field goal attempts and had three rebounds in 11 minutes. Luckily, he had a week to get cleared for Oklahoma's next contest on February 28, 2009, where he had 20 points and 18 rebounds in the team's 78-63 victory over Texas Tech on the road – a game where Griffin also collected a couple of assists and steals in the process.

Slowly but surely, Griffin was getting back to form late in the season as the team was able to have him back to form by March. In the team's March 7, 2009 game against Oklahoma State, Griffin had 33 points off of 12 field goals out of 15 attempts (80 percent) in an 82-78 win. Griffin also collected a total of 19 rebounds, 15 of which were on defense. The victory gave the Sooners a 13-3 conference record, which was the second best behind the Kansas Jayhawks (14-2).

Oklahoma would enter the conference tournament as one of the favorites to win, but they would be defeated by rival Oklahoma State Cowboys in the first game of the Big 12 conference tournament on March 12, 2009, which was eventually won by Missouri for the automatic bid in the NCAA National Championship tournament. Griffin would finish with making six out of his nine field goals for 17 points while collecting 19 rebounds. But it was a pair of late free throws from James Anderson that gave the Cowboys the one-point lead with less than three seconds left in the game.

It was a tough loss for the Sooners, but Oklahoma's bigger goal was the national title and their 27-5 overall slate was still good enough to earn them a No. 2 seeding in the South Region of the NCAA tournament. On March 19, 2009, Oklahoma would go on to rout Morgan State in their opening round encounter by a score of 82-54. Griffin would shoot 91.7 percent from the field (11 out of 12), and despite making six out of 10 from the free throw line, he finished with 28 points, 13 rebounds, two assists, and one steal.

On March 21, 2009, Griffin would put up 33 points and collect 17 rebounds in their second-round triumph over the Michigan Wolverines, 73-63. Griffin also had three assists, a blocked shot, and one steal for an overall well-rounded game for the Oklahoma star. The momentum would continue on March 27, 2009, when they eliminated Syracuse in the Sweet Sixteen, 84-71 to become the top-five-ranked team in the nation. Griffin had 30 points after shooting 80 percent from the field (12 out of 15), while collecting 14 rebounds, three assists, and one steal. The Sooners looked like they could be one of the stronger teams in the country.

However, in the Elite Eight on March 29, 2009, the University of North Carolina Tar Heels were the first seed in the South Region. This was the school that produced Michael Jordan, and that year's Tar Heel squad featured Ty Lawson, Danny Green, and Tyler Hansbrough. Griffin performed well with 23 points off of nine out of 12 field goals and 16 rebounds, but it wasn't enough as the Sooners lost to Griffin's draft batch mate Hansbrough and the Tar Heels, 72-60. While the focus was on the potential one-on-one matchup between Hansbrough and Griffin, the UNC captain would allow his teammates to win the game as Lawson and Green had 19 and 18 points respectively.

The loss provided an ending to the Sooners' dreams of winning the national crown and finished with a 30-6 record overall. North Carolina would go on to win the national championship after defeating Michigan State,

89-72, on April 6, 2009 at Ford Field in Detroit, Michigan.

But Griffin still had an amazing season averaging 22.7 points, 14.4 rebounds, and 2.3 assists per game during the regular season and was named to the All-American First Team. He also set school and Big 12 single-season records for most rebounds (504), rebounding average (14.4), double-doubles (30), and free throw attempts (324, the highest by a Sooner in a single season. With a total of 30 double-doubles during the year, he was just one shy of the NCAA record of 31 set by David Robinson in 1986–87. His total of 504 caroms were the most in a season by an NCAA Division I player since NBA legend Larry Bird had 505 in 1978–1979, and his rebounding average of 14.4 was the highest since Tim Duncan's 14.7 norm in 1996–1997.

Blake's older brother, Taylor, was performing as well between his junior year in the 2007-2008 season –

having an average of 6.5 points, 4.9 rebounds, and just under one assist per game. But then the 2008-2009 season provided one of Taylor's best statistical stat lines on his senior year – 9.6 points, 5.8 rebounds, and 1.3 assists per game.

For his sophomore year, Blake swept all the college post-season accolades. He was a no-brainer pick for Big 12 Player of the Year and was a unanimous choice by voters in all geographical districts for the Oscar Robertson Trophy. Likewise, he was named College Basketball Player of the Year by the *Associated Press*, getting 66 of the 71 national media panel members' votes. Furthermore, Griffin was announced as the winner of the prestigious Naismith College Player of the Year on April 5 in Detroit. Three days after turning pro, he won the John Wooden Award as college basketball's top player. He became the first Oklahoma player in school history to win the Naismith Award, Oscar Robertson Trophy, Adolph Rupp Trophy, John Wooden Award, and the *Associated Press* player of the year. In addition, he was also named Player of the Year by the Big 12, *Sports Illustrated*, *The Sporting News,* and FoxSports.com.

Blake declared for the NBA draft after his sophomore season. He announced his decision on a nationally televised press conference with his coach, Jeff Capel, on April 7, 2009. It was a choice coach Capel called a "no-brainer," with Griffin establishing himself as the most likely candidate to be the No. 1 overall pick in the draft due to his dominant college season and the relative lack of upper tier talent in the class. In his interview, he said, "I felt in my mind, from the time that I actually thought about it, that this would be the right decision. I remember talking to Coach Capel last year after I made my decision of coming back and he said I had the chance to be in this position and I should take it."

Chapter 4: Blake's NBA Career

There aren't a lot of soon-to-be rookies in the National Basketball Association who are going to have a nationally broadcasted announcement about their entrance into the league's rookie draft. But after two years at Oklahoma, Blake made his future public that he would leave college basketball. But before the draft, the NBA had to decide the order of the draft using a lottery.

The Los Angeles Clippers finished tied with the Washington Wizards for the second worst overall record in the previous NBA season with a 19-63 win-loss slate. There hadn't been a lot of success for the Clippers franchise in the years leading up to Blake Griffin's NBA arrival. They were even considered the B team that played home games at the Staples Center in Los Angeles.

During the draft lottery, they only had the third best odds at landing the first selection, as they lost a tiebreaker with the Wizards. However, the luck of the draw favored them as they won the lottery along with the opportunity to select a potential franchise player.

As expected, the Clippers tabbed Griffin with the first overall pick in the 2009 NBA Draft. The Clippers, at this point, were a moribund franchise. Most people regard them as the team that shares their home games with the Lakers. People even discouraged Griffin to play for the team, suggesting he should immediately request to be traded. Blake wouldn't listen to them, and he embraced the challenge of being the franchise's savior. The team showed their utmost trust and confidence in him that they traded away erstwhile starting power forward Zach Randolph to Memphis, so that they would be able to clear a spot for Griffin in the starting lineup.

Now, the first overall selection in the NBA Draft's history has a mixed amount of success. There have been guys like LeBron James, Tim Duncan, Glenn

Robinson, and Shaquille O'Neal. All of them had very respectful years that include several NBA Championships between all of them. But then, there are a number of first round selections who have a number of injury problems that caused their inability to truly realize the full potential that many experts had predicted they could have had. These players include Yao Ming, who was unable to remain healthy, having several different leg issues. Derrick Rose might also be joining that list as he had missed hundreds of games in the past few seasons.

Griffin got off to a fast start, winning the Summer League MVP by playing five games where he averaged about 19.2 points per game along with 10.8 rebounds and 3.2 assists as part of an overall performance where he made 50 percent of his field goals. Playing as a center for the Clippers' summer squad in Las Vegas, Blake had 27 points and 12 rebounds in his first game against the Los Angeles Lakers. He also had 16 points, eight rebounds, and four assists against the Phoenix Suns and his older brother Taylor. Many experts have found that the Sooner-turned-Clipper was showing quite a passion, despite only playing in exhibition games that have no meaning towards the season that starts in October.

After only five games against other young NBA players, Blake was displaying what many considered a total package with a combination of his ability to use his power for both scoring inside the paint, and muscling-out opponents to get rebounds on the defensive side of the court.

Therefore, it wasn't a surprise to see him on the Summer League's First Team along with Marcus Williams (Memphis Grizzlies), Chase Budinger (Houston Rockets), Anthony Randolph (Golden State Warriors), and Gary Forbes (NBA D-League). It was no surprise that the Clippers' summer league games attracted a lot of people throughout the entire organization, including the owner, Donald Sterling,

Coach Mike Dunleavy, and his future teammates, Baron Davis and Marcus Camby – all were happy to see the newest player to join them for the 2009-2010 NBA season.

During the pre-season, Blake continued the high level of play by averaging 13.7 points and 8.1 rebounds per game. Blake was all set to make his regular season debut with plenty of excitement. But during his final pre-season game against the New Orleans Hornets on October 26, 2009, he broke his left kneecap after dunking.

The original diagnosis was that he would only miss six weeks, but after that timeframe, tests revealed that his knee did not heal as expected. The highlight of his season was him being subjected to the traditional "rookie hazing" by his veteran teammates, making him sport a *Dora The Explorer* backpack and wear a light blue tuxedo two sizes too small. The franchise decided to play it safe with their prized asset, and his season was over before it began on January 20, 2010, when he underwent surgery on his left knee. It just felt par for the course after the team only had 19 wins and had a total of only two winning seasons in the prior three decades – with just one appearance in the playoffs in 1984. Although the team still had Davis, Camby, and veteran, Chris Kaman, there were a lot of hopes for Blake to join the team for a better squad.

The eternally star-crossed Clippers and their fans felt that they were doomed again. There were even fears that Blake could go down on the same path as another former number one pick, Greg Oden, who also sat out his rookie year and never fully recovered from his injuries to reach his potential. The Clippers themselves had a similar experience, as their own former highly-touted first round pick Shaun Livingston dislocated his left knee and tore every ligament in it during the 2006-2007 season. Livingston was never the same player he was before the injury.

Needless to say, when a top-level rookie joins the team and starts to have some major injury issues off the bat, the fans start to get negative quick. But sometimes, the best way to remedy that negativity is to see the results of what could be positive – although no one could really see that at the time as the Clippers continued to struggle in the 2009-2010 NBA season.

In the end, the Clippers slightly improved record-wise. They had a final record of 29-53, where they avoided last place. However, head coach Mike Dunleavy was fired after a record of 21-28 and Kim Hughes took over on an interim basis – but he didn't fare much better. In fact, he had only eight wins in 33 games to end the 2009-2010 season. A lot of Clippers fans were not pleased at all and were very fearful of the future as Vinny del Negro would be named the team's new head coach.

Those fears would be put to rest as Blake would go on to have a phenomenal first season in the league.

Although still considered a rookie after he didn't play a single game the previous year, he certainly didn't play like one. Blake had an impressive regular season debut as he scored 20 points and pulled down 14 rebounds in a losing effort against the Portland Trail Blazers, 98-88, on October 27, 2010. This was a prelude of things to come.

A few weeks later, Blake would make 11 out of 16 field goals to score 26 points and collect 10 rebounds for the Clippers in a losing effort, 111-104, to the Denver Nuggets on November 5, 2010. Later that month, Blake had an early career high with 44 points after shooting 58.3 percent from the field (14 out of 24) in a 124-115 loss to the New York Knicks on November 20, 2010. Additionally, Blake had 15 rebounds, seven assists, two steals, and one blocked shot in one of his most well-rounded games. However, at this point, the Clippers only had one win in their first 14 games despite Blake shooting just under 50 percent from the field, and averaging 18.5 points, 10.9 rebounds, and 2.1 assists.

Griffin would set a franchise record for most consecutive double-doubles with 23 as he totaled 23 points and 12 rebounds in a 105-91 win against the Golden State Warriors. His streak would end at 27 games on January 19, 2011 in a win against the Minnesota Timberwolves. This was the longest rookie double-double streak since 1968. He also became the first rookie with two 40+ point games in a season since Allen Iverson during the 1996-1997 campaign, breaking the barrier twice. The first was with a 44-point outburst against the New York Knicks then, the other one, setting his career-high of 47 in a win over the Indiana Pacers on January 17, 2011.

His performances impressed coaches so much that he was named a reserve on the 2011 Western Conference All-Star team. He became the first rookie to play in the All-Star game since Yao Ming was voted in 2003, and the first to be named by the coaches after Tim Duncan in 1997. He also participated in the Rookie Challenge and achieved his landmark jumping over a car win of the Slam Dunk Contest that helped him win the overall contest after defeating JaVale McGee (Washington Wizards), DeMar DeRozan (Toronto Raptors), and Serge Ibaka (Oklahoma City Thunder). Blake had a total score of 95 out of 100 between, and while McGee had the most points, Blake had led the voting 68 to 32 percent over McGee.

In the NBA All-Star Game on February 20, 2011 at the Staples Center, the Western Conference defeated the Eastern Conference 148-143. Blake had a lot of success with only 15 minutes by making four out of his six field goal attempts for eight points in addition to five rebounds and five assists. However, the MVP award for the All-Star Game went to Kobe Bryant of the Los Angeles Lakers with 37 points and 14 rebounds.

After being with the best in the NBA, Blake returned to the Clippers and the team would continue to struggle. However, he was doing very well, individually, despite the struggles to get wins. In the first game back from the All-Star Break, Griffin had 28 points on nine of 15 field goals with 11 rebounds and eight assists for a near-triple-double on February 22, 2011 in a 111-88 loss to the Oklahoma City Thunder. Getting double figures in three statistical categories is never an easy task, but Blake was able to get close many times throughout the season. On March 5, 2011, Blake was extremely close with nine assists in addition to his 18 points and 12 rebounds in the team's 100-94 home win over the Denver Nuggets.

He would reach that goal a few weeks later as he would register his first career triple-double with a 33-point, 17-rebound and 10-assist performance on March 23, 2011 in a double-overtime victory against the Washington Wizards, 127-119. As that was an amazing performance, Blake would add another triple-double in the final game of the season on April 13, 2011 at home against the Memphis Grizzlies. This time, he finished with 31 points, 10 rebounds, and 10 assists.

Something might have rubbed off on Blake during the All-Star Break. He would have a strong 26-game run to end the season with 21.9 points per game, as well as averages of 11 rebounds, four-and-a-half assists, and one steal.

Like his final college season, Blake would sweep all the awards available for a rookie after his remarkable year. He won all the Western Conference Rookie of the Month honors, making him the first one since his future teammate, Chris Paul, did it in 2003. He was able to play in all 82 games and he would finish with season averages of 22.5 points and 12.1 rebounds. Again, this was the first since former Clipper, Elton Brand, did it in the 1999-2000 season. He also led all rookies in points, rebounds, and double-doubles, and was the unanimous winner of the Rookie of the Year award, yet another first since David Robinson in 1990. Griffin was the only unanimous selection in the All-Rookie First Team. The media also recognized his sensational rookie-year efforts with *Sports Illustrated* listing him as one of the "NBA's 15 Greatest Rookies of All Time". The only moot point was that the Clippers failed to enter the playoffs, ending up with a mediocre 30-52 record. This means the team was more in the middle of the pack, away from the larger amount of balls that are entered for teams near the bottom of the standings wanting to get a higher selection in the upcoming rookie draft's order.

In some ways, with the mediocre record, the Clippers seem destined to their hard luck ways again as Cleveland won the 2011 NBA draft lottery with the first-round pick that originally belonged to them. The Cavaliers obtained it from an earlier trade that netted them long-time Clipper, Baron Davis, and that selection in exchange for veteran point guard, Mo

Williams, and forward Jamario Moon. Their long-suffering fans bemoaned this turn of events, but would be ecstatic with another off-season transaction that would take place later that year. However, the offs-season would last a lot longer than many expected.

When the 2005 Collective Bargaining Agreement (CBA) expired on 12:01 AM Eastern Daylight Time of July 1, 2011, a lockout began as there was no new deal in place before the deadline. This was the fourth work stoppage in league history, and the first since the 1998-1999 season. The main issues that divided the players and owners were revenue sharing and salary cap structure. During the lockout, NBA teams could not sign, trade, or contact players and, in turn, the players were denied access to their team's facilities and staff members. Negotiations between the owners led by now retired commissioner David Stern and the players, represented by director, Billy Hunter, and players' union president, Derek Fisher, stalled until November 26, 2011, when both sides were able to reach a tentative agreement. As a result, all pre-season games were canceled and the regular season was shortened to 66 games from its original length of 82.

The deal was finally ratified on December 8. Training camps, trades, and free agency began the next day. The short off-season period began with a bang when the Los Angeles Lakers, Houston Rockets, and the temporarily league-owned New Orleans Hornets announced that they had agreed to a trade-in principle that would have sent All-NBA point guard Chris Paul to the Lakers. Commissioner Stern, however, vetoed the deal explaining that the Hornets would be better off keeping Paul. This decision caused uproar around the league as everyone voiced their opinions on the matter. Star players, such as Dwyane Wade called the situation a "mess" to retired legends, such as Magic Johnson, who chimed in that the trade denial "sends a bad message to fans." The three teams lobbied for the deal to push through, but were met with resistance from the other owners who claimed it was an act of bad faith to the newly approved CBA. The frustrated Lakers finally pulled out of the trade talks. Their loss was their cross-town rivals' gain, as the Clippers moved in with an offer deemed acceptable by Stern. On December 14, 2011 the Clippers acquired Paul and two future second-round picks in exchange for Eric Gordon, Chris Kaman, Al-Farouq Aminu, and the Clips' 2012 first-round selection previously obtained from the Minnesota Timberwolves. The Clippers also signed free agents Caron Butler and Chauncey Billups. The disappointment of missing out on the first overall pick was replaced with utter joy. Blake Griffin would share the excitement as he exclaimed when he first found out about the news, "Yeah! It's going to be lob city!" Thus, the nickname was born.

"Lob City" got off the ground quickly as Paul energized the Clips' offense, transforming it to one of the most fast-paced and electric in the league. In the first game of the stoppage-shortened season, the Clippers defeated the Golden State Warriors on

December 25, 2011, 105-86. Griffin led the team with 22 points after making 9 out of 18 field goals, followed by 21 points from Chauncey Billups, and 20 points from his new teammate, Paul. Griffin would get the first of several double-doubles after scoring 34 points and 13 rebounds on December 30, 2011 in a 114-101 loss at home. It was one of only a few early losses as the team went 12-6 through January. February started off strong as well when Blake had 31 points off 14 of 22 field goal shooting (63.6 percent) to go along with 14 rebounds in a 107-105 win over the Utah Jazz in Salt Lake City on February 1, 2012.

Griffin's field goal percentage was strong during this season as well. He made 75 percent of his field goals the next day against the Denver Nuggets, 66.7 percent on February 4, 2012 against the Washington Wizards and 54.5 percent against the Orlando Magic. Throughout the year, Griffin would continue his strong play, not only scoring inside the paint, but also as someone who was dominant on the boards. A perfect example was his first game with 20 rebounds on February 18, 2012 against the San Antonio Spurs. The 20 rebounds went along with 22 points off of 50 percent field goal shooting (9 out of 18) for Griffin, but the Clippers would fall in overtime 103-100.

Last year, Griffin was a reservist for the Western Conference in the NBA All-Star Game. But in his second official season in the league, he was one of the starters along with Clippers teammate, Chris Paul. Their performances for the first half of the season earned Griffin his first All-Star start alongside teammate Paul, who was named an All-Star for the fourth time. It was the first time in franchise history that the team had two players start in the All-Star game. The starting lineup also included Kobe Bryant and Andrew Bynum of the crosstown-rival, Lakers, as the West defeated the East 152-149 on February 26, 2012 at Amway Center in Orlando, Florida. While Oklahoma City's Kevin Durant had 36 points and led the team, Griffin had 22 points after shooting 9 out of

12 field goals – including one from behind the three-point line – to go along with eight rebounds, three assists and two steals. The Clippers were now truly on the "league's map", as Blake put it earlier in the season. Griffin was also selected as "Team Shaq's" first pick in the inaugural Rising Stars Challenge, which replaced the traditional rookies versus sophomores' game.

Before the All-Star Weekend, however, the Clippers' bubble burst when Chauncey Billups was lost for the season after tearing his Achilles' tendon. His absence was felt, as the team would lose 12 of the succeeding 19 games, jeopardizing the job of their head coach Vinny del Negro. Just like their fortunes before the season, the team would turn it around by winning 12 of their next 14, including victories over defending champion, Dallas, and another Western Conference powerhouse, the Oklahoma City Thunder. The team also added veteran forward, Kenyon Martin, in February and flamboyant guard, Nick Young, in

March for added offensive firepower and to augment Billups' loss.

In that run, nearing the end of the shortened regular season, Blake was shooting just under 60 percent from the field while scoring an average of 19 points, 10.9 rebounds, and 4.1 assists. Griffin's game remained strong on rebounding from the boards during this run. This impressive run resulted in the Clippers making the playoffs for the first time since 2006, finishing with a 40-26 slate, which was good enough for them to earn the fifth seed in the loaded West.

The Clippers faced Griffin's predecessor and later arch-nemesis, Zach Randolph, and the Memphis Grizzlies in the first round of the 2011 playoffs. They would win a bruising and hard-fought series in seven games. In the first game of the series, Griffin and Paul were able to combine for 31 points, 11 rebounds and 12 assists to get the edge in a 99-98 win on April 29, 2012 at the FedEx Forum in Memphis, Tennessee. The

Grizzlies were able to tie the series in Game 2 on May 2, 2012 with Rudy Gay (20 points) and O. J. Mayo (20 points) leading the way, despite Paul's 29 points and Griffin's 22 points to lead the team.

At the Staples Center, the Clippers were able to take advantage of the home court with an 87-86 victory during Game 3 on May 6, 2012. Paul was able to lead the team with 24 points and 11 rebounds, while Griffin provided additional support with 17 points for 32 minutes of playing time. Griffin would have a much better performance in Game 4 on May 7, 2012 for 101-97 win in overtime to give the Clippers a 2-1 series lead. Griffin led all players with 30 points after making 10 out of 15 field goals to go along with seven assists and five rebounds. However, he would struggle in Games 5 and 6 with only 15 points and 11 rebounds in a 92-80 loss on May 9, 2012, and just 17 points in a 90-88 loss at the Staples Center on May 11, 2012.

The Clippers were able to complete an amazing comeback from an early deficit in Game 7 on May 13, 2012 in Memphis to beat the Grizzlies 82-72 on their home court. Griffin, however, only had eight points but with the points contributed by his teammates, Paul (19 points), Nick Young (13 points), and Kenyon Martin (11 points), the Los Angeles Clippers move on to the Western Conference playoffs. However, the Clippers' inexperience would be their downfall in the next round as the veteran laded San Antonio Spurs sent them crashing back to earth with a four-game series sweep. Nevertheless, it was the season that saw the return of the Clippers to league relevance.

Despite the sweep, Griffin looked strong as he averaged 21 points, 7.8 rebounds, 2.3 assists, two blocked shots, and a little more than one steal per game. He also had a 46.8 field goal percentage and an 80 percent conversion rate for his free throws. Even though Blake's averages dipped to 20.7 points and 10.9 rebounds, he was named to the All-NBA Second

Team along with Kevin Love (Minnesota Timberwolves), Andrew Bynum (Los Angeles Lakers), Tony Parker (San Antonio Spurs), and Russell Westbrook (Oklahoma City Thunder). He was also chosen to play for Team USA in the 2012 London Olympics, but he withdrew when he injured his knee during practice.

Recognized as the man who was hugely responsible for the team's turnaround, former Clippers general manager, Neil Olshey, was hired by conference rival, the Portland Trail Blazers. The then new Clippers general manager, Gary Sacks, didn't waste any time making his own imprint on the team and signed Blake for a 5-year contract extension reportedly worth $95 million. He then made further moves in order to improve the Clippers' chances of making a playoff run in the incoming 2012-2013 campaign. The team reacquired forward Lamar Odom during the 2012 NBA draft. This was followed by the acquisition of sixth-man extraordinaire Jamal Crawford and the resigning of Chauncey Billups, who has a few NBA Championships under his belt during his time with the Detroit Pistons. The Clippers would wrap up their offseason shopping and bringing in the likes of former All-Star, Grant Hill, centers, Ryan Hollins and Ronny Turiaf, shooting guard, Willie Green, and rugged forward, Matt Barnes. With these acquisitions, the Clippers had their best line-up in years and were poised to improve on their return to the playoffs from the previous year and make further progress and, perhaps, even a shot for the NBA championship glory.

The regular season started as planned. The Clippers won 17 straight games from the end of November to the whole month of December, setting franchise records for both their time in Buffalo, when they were known as the Braves, and their present day location in Los Angeles. They also became just the third NBA team to record an undefeated month. At that time, Griffin was averaging 18.6 points and 8.7 rebounds while Paul was around 16.4 points and 9.4 assists per game during this franchise record winning streak. One of Griffin's best games during this stretch was on December 3, 2012 when he made 30 points after 14 out of 20 field goals with 11 rebounds in a 105-104 win over the Utah Jazz. It was the Denver Nuggets that ended the streak on January 2, 2013. One week later, the Clippers would set another franchise record with their 13th consecutive home game win, with a 99-93 victory over Dallas where Griffin had 15 points and 13 rebounds while Paul led the team with 19 points and 16 assists.

Prior to the All-Star Break, Griffin was showing much improved defensive awareness as he had four steals in four different games – December 8, 2012 against the Pheonix Suns; December 23, 2012, while visiting the Suns; January 26, 2013 against the Portland Trail Blazers, and; February 13, 2013 against the Houston Rockets.

Blake and Chris were again at the forefront of the team's success, and both were named All-Star game starters for the second year running. On February 17, 2013 at the Toyota Center in Houston, Texas, the Western Conference would once again defeat the Eastern Conference, 143-138. Both Clippers stars were on the starting rotation along with two Lakers (Bryant and Dwight Howard). Griffin was effective on that game making 9 out of 11 field goals for 19 points to go along with three rebounds, three assists, two steals, and one block. Griffin recorded his third career triple-double with 23 points, 11 rebounds, and 11 assists on March 6, 2013, leading the Clippers to triumph over the Milwaukee Bucks with a score of 117-101.

The Clippers were reaching a number of firsts on this season, thanks to the recent upgrades to help support the stars, Griffin and Paul. On April 3, 2013, the Clippers notched their 50th victory, another franchise best, in a 126-101 rout of the Phoenix Suns – a game where Griffin didn't do much with only nine points, seven assists and five rebounds. Three days later, they swept the season series with the Lakers, capturing their first Pacific division title in the process – Griffin and Paul each scored 24 points in the game while Griffin had 12 rebounds and Paul had 12 assists.

They finished with a 56-26 record and the fourth seed in the conference, an improvement over last year in terms of record and seeding. This also gave the Clippers something they hadn't won in a very long time, the Pacific Division – which was perennially held by the other Los Angeles team for more than a decade.

The Clippers once again faced the Memphis Grizzlies in the first round of the 2013 playoffs. They won the first two games that started with a 112-91 win on April 20, 2013 at home thanks to Paul's 23 points. He was also the star in Game 2 as he hit the buzzer beater for the 93-91 win – the two biggest of Paul's 24 points – to give the Clippers an early series advantage. Griffin also had a much stronger performance after the 10 points in Game 1. He had 21 points, eight rebounds, and four assists to support Paul's big game.

However, the Grizzlies turned the tables on them, winning four straight games and taking the series win, four games to two. The season that started so brightly for the Clippers ended abruptly without warning. Griffin, who had a mediocre season, was unable to continue his performance from the previous season's success with averages of 12 points, five rebounds, and two assists during those four losses in the Western Conference playoffs against Memphis.

Griffin's averages further dropped to career worst norms to 18.0 points and 8.3 rebounds. Although he was again a member of the All-NBA Second Team, it is an undeniable fact that this was his most disappointing season to-date. However, the dip in numbers didn't exactly mean a regression in his game, as he also averaged a career-low in minutes played.

Blake would later on surmise that he felt it was part of Del Negro's ploy not to rely too much on his starters and get the bench more involved.

It didn't work for Del Negro as the Clippers declined to renew his contract following their premature exit from the playoffs – even though the team had reached a franchise record in wins and a rare division title. In a rare occurrence, the Clippers acquired championship-winning coach Glenn "Doc" Rivers from the Boston Celtics in exchange for a 2015 unprotected first-round pick. Rivers was also given the title of Senior Vice President of Basketball Operations. The Celtics decided to let go of him because he wasn't eager to stick around to rebuild their aging team as revered veterans, Paul Pierce and Kevin Garnett, would also follow Rivers to the exit door.

The fast-rising Clippers presented more of a welcome challenge for Rivers. They continued to tinker with their roster. They traded away young stud guard, Eric

Bledsoe, and veteran, Caron Butler, to the Phoenix Suns, getting in return shooters, Jared Dudley and J.J. Redick (from Milwaukee). The team felt that they had to space the floor to give Griffin more operating room in the post. On July 7, 2013, they re-signed Ryan Hollins, Matt Barnes, and, most importantly, locked-up Chris Paul to a 5-year contract extension. They also signed free agent Darren Collison to fill-up the back-up point guard role vacated by the departures of Bledsoe and Chauncey Billups, who returned to the Detroit Pistons, the team he previously won a championship with.

The appointment of Doc Rivers would be a boon to Blake's game, as he averaged a career-high of 24.1 points during the 2013-2014 regular season. A lot of this had to do with having two games with more than 40 points and 16 total games where he would score at least 30 points. One of Griffin's best individual performances was during a 116-112 loss to the Miami Heat on February 5, 2014, where he had 43 points after shooting 16 out of 34 field goals and made 10 out of 17 free throws – this went along with 15 rebounds and six assists. This game was about just under two months after Griffin scored 40 points and 10 rebounds in the Clippers' 98-90 win at home over the Utah Jazz on December 28, 2013.

Another contributing factor to the uptick in his scoring was that he had added responsibility in carrying the offense while Paul missed almost a month of games to a shoulder injury. During this 18-game stretch, Griffin had averaged 27.5 points per game along with 8.2 rebounds, 4.4 assists for an average playing time of 35 minutes per game during this period. In addition to his 43-point game against the Heat, Griffin had another high-quality game, having 36 points, 11 rebounds, and five assists in a 116-115 loss to the Denver Nuggets on February 3, 2014.

It was no surprise that Griffin made the All-Star team for the fourth straight time as a starter for the third consecutive year. On February 16, 2014, at the Smoothie King Center in New Orleans, Louisiana, Griffin was one of the main starters and earned his spot with 38 points (tied with Oklahoma City's Kevin Durant) to go along with six rebounds. However, the Eastern Conference would get the win over the West by a score of 163-155.

The Clippers would again make additions to their team before the trade deadline, making moves for forwards, Glen Davis and Danny Granger, for more depth. By this time, Blake had scored an average of 20 points or more in a span of a franchise record of 31 straight games from January 20 to March 26. On March 6, 2014, the Clippers humiliated their cross-town rivals, the Lakers, walloping them by 48 points, 142-94, their largest margin of victory and the Lakers' most lopsided loss. On April 2, 2014, the Clippers defeated Phoenix, 112-108, to clinch their second consecutive division title. Griffin then recorded his fourth career triple-double the following day as he wound up with

25 points, 10 rebounds, and 11 assists in a losing cause to Dallas. The Clippers improved their franchise best, finishing with a 57-25 record and garnering the third seed in the West.

This time around, the Clippers were pitted against division rival, Golden State Warriors, which was another rising team in the conference. The Warriors presented a different challenge, with their high-octane offense revolving around the dynamic scoring backcourt duo, Stephen Curry and Klay Thompson, collectively known as the "Splash Brothers". They were a change of pace from the physical, ground and pound style of their former tormentors, Memphis. The Warriors took the first game on April 19, 2014, with 109-105. But the Clippers were able to bounce back in the series' second game where Griffin had 35 points after making 13 out of 17 of his field goals (76.5 percent).

Griffin would follow-up that performance by scoring a playoff best of 32 points in Game 3 to put the Clippers in the driving seat, two games to one – defeating the Warriors 98-96 on April 24, 2014. It also helped that his teammate, DeAndre Jordan, led the team with 22 rebounds. However, it was a short lived victory as the Clippers found themselves in a little bit of controversy off the court.

A day after, the team's owner Donald Sterling was embroiled in controversy for making racist remarks. Sterling already had a reputation for racist behavior dating back to the 1990s. Entertainment news website *TMZ* released a taped conversation between Sterling and former lover, V. Stiviano, wherin he reprimanded her for associating herself with black people in an *Instagram* photo, including NBA legend, Magic Johnson, saying he didn't want them to be present at the Clippers' games. An unprecedented backlash followed with some of the Clippers' sponsors, such as Kia (which Griffin endorses), State Farm Insurance, and Virgin America severing ties with them. Many also threatened to boycott the team, egging the players to do the same.

The Clippers' players protested the remarks of their owner instead by wearing their shirts inside out during pregame warm-ups in Game 4, hiding their team name and logo. The Warriors took advantage of this unwelcome distraction by tying the series in Game 4 and won, 118-97, on April 27, 2014.

After a league investigation, the tape was proven to be authentic and the NBA handed Donald Sterling the severest of penalties – a lifetime ban, and a fine of $2.5 million. Commissioner Adam Silver also forced Sterling to sell the team. Relieved that this was all behind them, the Clippers would go on to win the back-and-forth thriller of a series in seven games. Griffin led them with 24 points in Game 7, while DeAndre Jordan grabbed 18 rebounds, and Chris Paul orchestrating the offense with 14 assists.

The Clippers moved on to the second round against Kevin Durant, Russell Westbrook, and the Oklahoma City Thunder, who took care of the Clips' former rivals, Memphis, also in seven games. The series was tied two games apiece, which started with 23 points from Griffin in the Clippers' 122-105 win in Oklahoma City. After struggles in Games 2 and 3, Griffin had 25 points and nine rebounds in the near double-double to help Los Angeles get the 101-99 win on May 11, 2014. But the Thunder would take the next two games and the series. Once again, Griffin and the Clippers fell short of their ultimate goal.

Coming off his finest year, Blake finished third in the regular season MVP voting behind perennial award contenders LeBron James and first-time winner, Kevin Durant. Curiously, he only made the All-NBA Second Team despite averaging 24.1 points per game in a season where he had 43 double-doubles for a total of 80 games.

The Clippers' ownership situation was resolved on May 27, 2014. Former Microsoft chief executive officer, Steve Ballmer, purchased the team for two billion dollars. He beat out competition from Oprah Winfrey, Floyd Mayweather, and Magic Johnson. Blake said in an article that he penned himself after this saga that he's just happy Sterling was gone, a sentiment likely shared by the rest of the organization. He praised new owner, Ballmer, saying that he wants to "win at all costs" and that the players "love his kind of crazy."

During this preseason and the first few games of the 2014-2015 regular season, Griffin has been displaying a marked improvement in his jump shot. In their preseason opener against the Warriors, Griffin made six straight jumpers, three from the corner and the other three from the elbow. A comparison of his shooting form from the previous season indicated that he is shooting with more confidence. He gets into his rhythm much sooner, which results to a more fluid release. A breakdown of his shooting motion last year showed that his stance was too wide when he received the ball and his motion was slower which led to a "choppier" shot. Over Fox Sports West, he said, "I'm just trying to be confident, take the shot and, miss or make, try to keep that aggressive mentality."

Griffin would start in only 67 out of the season's 82 regular season games but he would average 21.9 points per game, as well as 7.6 rebounds, 5.3 assists, and nearly one steal each night. There weren't any triple-doubles but Griffin was scoring a lot of points at some highlights of the season, including 45 points after making 14 out of 24 on December 8, 2014in an overtime thriller win against the Phoenix Suns at home, 121-120. The only other time Griffin would score 40 or more points was on March 31, 2015, in a 110-106 loss to the Golden State Warriors – a team that would be a thorn in their sides as the new breakout team in the NBA's Pacific Division. In this game, he scored 40 points after making 16 out of 25 field goals with 12 rebounds and five assists.

In addition to his scoring average being above 20 points per game, Griffin was also reaching better accuracy with several games with higher field goal percentages in his fifth official season in the NBA. On November 29, 2014, Griffin made 72.2 percent of his field goals (13 out of 18) to score 28 points in a 112-96 win over the Utah Jazz. A few months later, Griffin made 73.3 percent by making 11 of 15 shots for 22 points in a 120-100 victory over the Dallas Mavericks on January 10, 2015. Not even two weeks later, on January 22, 2015, the Clippers defeated the Brooklyn Nets, 123-84, thanks, in part, to Griffin making 11 out of 14 field goals (78.6 percent) for 24 points.

With how he continued to improve, it was of no surprise when Griffin would once again be voted as a starter for the Western Conference team for the 2015 NBA All-Star Game on February 15, 2015 at Madison

Square Garden in New York City, New York. The West was able to get some revenge from their loss last season by defeating the East, 163-158. However, even though he was selected to the team, Griffin was dealing with a right elbow injury.

That injury kept him out of action from early February to mid-March. Although it took a few games before getting back into his groove, Griffin had 40 points and 12 rebounds in a game against the Golden State Warriors on March 31, 2015. The season ended with the Clippers having a 56-26 record that was good enough for second place in the NBA's Pacific Division – behind the Golden State Warriors' 67-15 record. There were hopes that the Clippers could start to develop more as the main team for the city of Los Angeles, as the Lakers continued to go into a steady decline with only 21 wins in the 2014-15 season.

The first step for the Clippers was a series against the veteran-led San Antonio Spurs. Griffin had 26 points and 12 rebounds in a 107-92 win on April 19, 2015, to start the first round series. The Spurs were able to bounce back and tie the series in Game 2 with a 111-107 overtime win on April 22, 2015 despite Griffin's 29 points, 12 rebounds, and 11 assists to lead the Clippers. However, he wouldn't be able to maintain that performance as he only had 14 points in a 100-73 loss in San Antonio on April 24, 2015. This was followed by 20 points and 19 rebounds from Griffin that resulted to a Game 4 victory, 114-105, win on April 26, 2015. Despite the Spurs jumping ahead three games to two, the Clippers were able to earn two very close decisions with Griffin having 26 points and 12 rebounds in the team's 102-96 win on April 30, 2015. This was followed by 24 points, 13 rebounds, and 10 assists in a 111-109 win on May 2, 2015. It was a successful series where Griffin averaged nearly a triple-double with 24.1 points, 10.4 rebounds, and 7.4 assists.

Griffin's playoff performance would continue to grow stronger in the second round of the Western Conference playoffs against the Houston Rockets. On May 4, 2015, he started with 26 points, 14 rebounds, and 13 assists in a 117-101 win in Game 1. Griffin would have 34 points and 15 rebounds on defense despite the loss on Game 2 with a score of 115-109. However, Griffin and the Clippers would continue to play strong in Games 3 and 4. He had 22 points and 14 rebounds on May 8, 2015 in a 124-99 win. This was followed by 21 points to join DeAndre Jordan's 26 points to help the Clippers win and take the 3-1 series lead with a 128-95 win on May 10, 2015.

However, the Clippers would not be able to close out the series. They lost the fifth, sixth, and seventh games with the Rockets taking the series in Game 7 on May 17, 2015 with a score of 113-100. James Harden scored 31 points supported by Trevor Ariza's 22 points and Dwight Howard's 16 points. Despite the Clippers having the inability to close out the series, no one could blame Griffin after having higher averages in those three games of 28.3 points, 11.7 rebounds, and a 57.8 field goal percentage. The Rockets advanced to the Western Conference Finals before they lost to the eventual NBA Champions, Golden State, which defeated LeBron James and the Cleveland Cavaliers.

Having lower numbers than the previous years, Griffin had to settle for being selected to the All-NBA's Third Team – along with Clippers teammate, DeAndre Jordan, and a few other players like veteran, Tim Duncan (San Antonio Spurs), Klay Thompson (Golden State Warriors), and Kyrie Irving (Cleveland Cavaliers).

With the disappointment that took place in the 2014-15 NBA season, Griffin and the rest of the Clippers are hoping to improve their team's defense. In a recent story on ESPN.com in early October, Griffin stated that he was going to make an adjustment to the leadership of the team and will shift to a more physical style of play to compete with some of the league's best developing at Golden State and the Eastern Conference's Cleveland Cavaliers.

Head coach, Doc Rivers, stated in the same article that the expectations are the same, but that they are hoping for improved numbers. He said, "We've probably been on him more about defense." That statement might mean having to take away some of the power he uses towards his dunks and using that energy to be a better defender on the other side of the court. In the weeks leading up to the 2015-2016 NBA season, the Clippers are headed to China for a preseason trip for a few final exhibition games. As part of a marketing plan for Nike, Paul and Griffin will have an opportunity to make several appearances with NBA legend, Michael Jordan – someone who knows a thing or two about winning championships having won two three-peats of the NBA Finals with the Chicago Bulls during the 1990s. When you want to be one of the best teams in the league, you would want to learn from someone who had six NBA championships and five title reigns as the league's most valuable player award. He would be a great mentor for a team that wants to advance beyond the second round for the first time in the 46-year history of the Clippers' franchise.

If Griffin is able to improve his overall defense, and if some of the big names who joined the Clippers would step up, the Clippers just might rise to the top as what happened to the Golden State Warriors. Although the team lost Matt Barnes via trade, a major key to the Clippers' success will be the outcome of their acquisition of free agent, Paul Pierce, who is a former NBA champion with the Boston Celtics. Likewise, the acquisition of Josh Smith and Lance Stephenson will hopefully be able to support the Griffin-Paul duo known as "Lob City." Speaking with Jordan might just help, considering his six championships were, in part, the result of the partnership between Jordan and his Bulls teammate, Scottie Pippen while being supported by a cast, which includes Dennis Rodman, Horace Grant, and Steve Kerr.

Chapter 5: Griffin's Personal Life

Even though he plays in a city known for its glitz and glamor, Blake Griffin does not readily embrace the fame that someone like him attracts, unlike most of the so-called NBA "superstars". He doesn't go out partying after games, and is rarely spotted at celebrity gatherings. In an interview with *Slam* Magazine, he told Chris Palmer that, "I never wanted to be famous; I just wanted to play basketball."

Blake is still very close to his family. He looks up to his parents as his inspirations in life. "Both of my parents are two of the hardest working people I've honestly ever known in my life," he said. "They each worked two jobs throughout my brother's and my childhood. Just the way they live, they still do the exact same things they always did." His parents continue to live in the same house in Oklahoma since the Griffin brothers' childhood. He also recalled that it was his father, while coaching him, who taught him the importance of relying on his teammates. Blake told *The New York Post*, "My father taught me how to become multi-dimensional, to be more than just a scorer, rebounder and passer. He taught me how to make my teammates better." His parents watched a lot of the brothers' games when they were in college at Oklahoma due to its proximity to their house. Today, Blake still calls them regularly to check on their well-being.

Blake continues to enjoy a very close relationship with his brother, Taylor. He even credits Taylor for being his model for his work ethic. In fact, he mentioned in an interview with *GQ* magazine that he observed his brother as he went about his preparations for a game. According to Blake, Taylor was very meticulous and everything that he did – working out, shooting extra hoops, stretching, etc. – was for a reason.

Taylor was a senior when Blake was a sophomore at Oklahoma University, where the two were part of the

Sooners team that made the Elite Eight in the 2009 NCAA National Championship tournament. While Blake would move on to a great young career in the National Basketball Association, older brother Taylor didn't have the same success after being selected by the Phoenix Suns as the 48th overall selection in the 2009 NBA Draft. Taylor would make a total of eight appearances with the Suns in his rookie season but spent most of his time with the Iowa Energy of the NBA D-League.

Taylor was released from the team in the summer of 2010 and he would play with the Belgacom Liege Basket of Belgium. He would return to the NBA briefly after signing with the Charlotte Bobcats on December 10, 2011 – only to be released less than two weeks later. He then joined the Dakota Wizards in Bismark, North Dakota in their final season in the NBA D-League before the team folded. Taylor would then spend a few seasons, on and off due to injuries, with the Santa Cruz Warriors of the D-League, which he helped win the league championship on April 26, 2015. Currently, he is playing in the Italian Series A2 league with Pallacanestro Trapani.

Away from the basketball court, Blake is still active in life with his older brother. He goes with Taylor and his wife to a Bible study group when he has the time. They watch also NBA League Pass and play *ping-pong* in his house. On his 25th birthday last March, his brother's wife Marieka even baked Blake his favorite strawberry cake, just like his mother did for him his previous birthdays. This speaks of Blake's family values, and that his fame hasn't changed him with regards to this aspect.

Blake considers himself an Evangelical Christian. He and Taylor attended church almost every Sunday when they were young. Blake even said that his rookie season-ending injury was "God's way of humbling him" so he can have the proper attitude. In fact, he received serious flak when he declared in April 2014 that he believed in the Biblical creation as opposed to Charles Darwin's theory of evolution. "I was raised in a Christian household and went to a Christian high school," Blake told *Rolling Stone*, "so I believe in creationism." He never backtracked from his statements and shrugged off the heat he took from the likes of Bill Maher. He expounded further on why he believed in creationism. "I believe in science," he says. "I believe in all of that. I just…honestly, when I'm at the beach and I'm looking at the ocean, I'm looking at the mountains and the sun is setting, I'm seeing people running up and down, laughing, having fun, I'm like, 'This had to be created. This is created.' And that's my personal thing."

Three days before his milestone win in the 2011 NBA Slam Dunk Contest, Blake suffered a personal tragedy. His high school teammate and friend, Wilson Holloway, a football player at the University of Tulsa, succumbed to a battle with Hodgkin's lymphoma. Griffin found out after their game against the

Minnesota Timberwolves, and he was inconsolable at the Clippers' locker room. They were set to meet in an upcoming road game of the Clippers against Oklahoma City, Blake's hometown NBA team. Griffin donated the Kia that he jumped over in the dunk contest to the *Stand Up To Cancer* charity for Hodgkin's lymphoma research in memory of Holloway. "I am honored to memorialize Wilson's legacy by helping raise funds for cancer research," Griffin said in a statement. "Wilson was an inspiration to everybody who knew him, and a very dear friend and teammate." He also donates 100 dollars for each dunk he makes to fight childhood obesity, courtesy of the *Dunking for Dollars* charity.

A hobby and interest of Griffin is "punching up" jokes on scripts sent to him by his buddy Neal Brennan, a co-creator of *The Chappelle Show*. He has also developed a reputation for being a funny guy, having dry wit and a sense of humor to boot and his interviews are among the most entertaining. During the 2011 NBA lockout, he became an intern for comedy website, *Funny or Die*, co-founded by Will Ferrell and Adam McKay. He helped in writing, shooting and acting in some videos for the site. Griffin said that he wanted to learn more about film production, hence, the reason for his internship. He and teammate, DeAndre Jordan, on March 23, 2014 did a funny live script reading of *Space Jam* with some other comedians and cast members of *The League*. Griffin portrayed *His Airness* himself, Michael Jordan, who starred in the movie alongside the *Looney Tunes* cartoon characters. Blake also had a small part in Sacha Baron Cohen's *The Dictator*. One of his dunks was used in a scene where Baron Cohen thinks of it right before he climaxes.

On September 24, 2013, Blake became a father for the first time. He and Brynn Cameron, a former University of Southern California basketball player who also has a child with former NFL quarterback Matt Leinart, announced that they have had a healthy baby boy named Ford Wilson Cameron-Griffin. "We are very happy to have a healthy baby, but respectfully request to keep our personal affairs private and let us focus on parenting our son," Griffin said in a statement released to the *Los Angeles Times*.

Chapter 6: Impact on Basketball

What is a true measure of a basketball star's impact on the sport? Is it to become a cover-boy of an NBA game like the *NBA 2K13*, such as stars like Kevin Durant of the Oklahoma City Thunder and Derrick Rose of the Chicago Bulls, or of a college basketball game like *NCAA Basketball 10*? Or is it being able to receive one of several endorsement deals with big-name companies by helping promote products, such as Kia Motors vehicles, Subway sandwiches, or the newest television model from Vizio?

All of that helps reward a player for being able to act as a good role model both on and off the court, but it starts with being able to make a significant impact in the sport as one of the best in the league. While Blake Griffin has quite the personality to be in commercials and other forms of media, there's no denying how passionate he is about basketball. Just ask the shot clock one of his slam dunks tore down before a preseason game against the Toronto Raptors on October 4, 2015. Even before the official start of the 2015-2016 NBA season, the former Oklahoma Sooner is looking to be in mid-season form. His dunking prowess has been the primary source of his acclaim and, ironically, of his criticism also. On one side, fans and players alike have been awed by his superhuman-leaping ability and gravity-defying highlights and facial slams. NBA TV analyst and former Orlando Magic shooter, Dennis Scott, even dubbed him as "Must-See BG." His endorsement of the Jordan brand, famous for the player it was created for and its *jump man* logo is a mutually beneficial fit for both player and employer. On the other hand, naysayers have dismissed Griffin as a one-dimensional player, who only knows how to dunk and not much else. Leading this group is retired legend and current TNT analyst, Charles Barkley, who had, on many occasions, accused Griffin of being "soft" and of "flopping" all the time. He even suggested that Blake is an "overrated" player.

Because of this, Griffin has become a polarizing figure of sorts in the league, whether be it deservingly or not. He has become the player opponents love to hate or, at least, hate to play against. Some claim this is because of his perceived on-court arrogance, the attitude of, "I'm going to dunk on you no matter what", and also because of his refusal to dish out retaliation even if opponents resort to some underhanded tactics while defending him. The furthest that he has ever gone to was giving his enemies the "death stare". Even his own teammate, Matt Barnes, became fed-up of defending him from his assailants, saying it only cost him money in fines. The list of NBA players who have been involved in a sort of fracas with him are growing, and this includes Zach Randolph, Andrew Bogut, Serge Ibaka, and David Lee. Then Charlotte Bobcats forward, Josh McRoberts, said that he'd rather not talk about Griffin's physical play because he doesn't want to get "in trouble". His coach, Doc Rivers, has defended Griffin from his detractors pointing out that "Blake gets hit as much as anybody in the league and it gets old; I'm not going to say what I really want to say. I just think he's playing really well right now and some people don't like that." He may have said that because of the hits inflicted on Griffin, such as a groin shot from Ibaka and Phoenix bruiser P.J. Tucker's pulling him to the ground and elbowing him in the chest. Not all his contemporaries hate to play against him though. Some players, such as Nuggets forward and recent Team USA gold medal winner, Kenneth Faried, accept it as a challenge and even enjoys it.

The positive side in all of this is if they are talking about you the way they have discussed and dissected Blake Griffin's game, then you have made it big. He doesn't retaliate because he has learned to control himself from reactionary rage in these types of situations. This has been the reason why he has also been branded as "soft". But for his brother, Taylor,

Blake is doing all right. Taylor said that their early childhood battles taught Blake the importance of composure and not losing his cool. "You don't have to swing back," says Taylor, "but you have to stand your ground." Running mate, Chris Paul, agrees. "He could easily punch back and get to fighting," concurs Paul, "But no. I don't know how he does it. That's pretty selfless."

During this preseason, there was an incident where Blake Griffin wanted to pick a fight with Utah Jazz forward, Trevor Booker, after Booker committed a flagrant foul on him on a dunk attempt. It could be the start of his attempt to silence his doubters, or it could be just an isolated incident altogether, and he will return back to his extremely tolerant self.

Chapter 7: Blake Griffin's Legacy and Future

Blake Griffin is easily one of the most recognizable players in professional basketball today. From his daily appearances in highlight reels to his hilarious TV advertisements, his name and freckled face are known all over the world, especially in hoop crazy nations. He appeared on the cover of the popular NBA licensed game NBA2K13, along with fellow stars, Derrick Rose and Kevin Durant. He also has a deal with Panini America that features his autographs and memorabilia in their products.

Early in his career, Blake was made very popular by his signature dunks and athleticism. He has been affected by the criticism of his game, but now brushes it off, saying that he's become used to it. Blake has made strides in improving his post-game and his free-throw shooting. Griffin has also extended his range, becoming more accurate with the mid-range jumper and can now even make the occasional 3-pointer. If he proves that he is now a consistent shooter, it will lead to his evolution into a complete player and be compared to the great Karl Malone, one of the most complete power forwards in league history. He has also been recently commended as one of the current better-passing and facilitating big men in the game. In an early season matchup against the Lakers last October 31, these improvements in his game were in full display as he poured in 39 points and missed only one of his 12 free throws, powering his Clippers to a 117-111 win over the returning Kobe Bryant and a Laker squad still grasping their respective roles in the team. Griffin acknowledges that the Clippers can't overtake the Lakers as the favorite team in Los Angeles because of their immense history, but they intend to prove that they are the better team in LaLaland at the moment. It is somehow ironic that the state of these two franchises has seemingly been reversed from the time that Griffin and Chris Paul were obtained by the Clippers, as the Lakers are now the ones struggling to find their identity with only Kobe and another basketball phenomenon, Jeremy Lin, among their roster that could be considered as household names.

Griffin's immense potential and vastly improving game has everyone wondering how far he can go. Is an MVP award on the horizon? Could he and Chris Paul finally lead the Clippers to the promise land? Fantasy basketball owners have also invested heavily on him this season, many believing it to be the season where he claims his place among the NBA's elite. When asked by *GQ* on what his plans are after he retires, Blake said that he wants to be an intern in a production company and not be involved in basketball anymore. If he continues to display his relentless work ethic combined with his God-given ability, he won't be able to do that anytime soon.

Griffin could be one of the best all-around players who can easily earn triple-doubles multiple times throughout the rest of his career. It's a dangerous thing to consider a player who might be able to develop a stronger sense of defense and possibly get more blocked shots and maybe force a few more steals on the average. However, Griffin could pose as a more complete prototype for a perfect type of player for the NBA. If he is able to do this, who knows what level the Clippers might ascend to. They could reach the level that their division rivals, the Golden State Warriors, achieved in 2015 and, maybe eventually, a level that the Lakers did about 10 years ago. It could even possibly be the level that Jordan's Bulls did 10 years before that. Only the future holds the answer to what lies ahead for Blake Griffin and the LA Clippers. No matter what, Blake will definitely be something worth watching out for.

Final Word/About the Author

I was born and raised in Norwalk, Connecticut. Growing up, I could often be found spending many nights watching basketball, soccer, and football matches with my father in the family living room. I love sports and everything that sports can embody. I believe that sports are one of most genuine forms of competition, heart, and determination. I write my works to learn more about influential athletes in the hopes that from my writing, you the reader can walk away inspired to put in an equal if not greater amount of hard work and perseverance to pursue your goals. If you enjoyed *Blake Griffin: The Inspiring Story of One of Basketball's Most Dominant Power Forwards* please leave a review! Also, you can read more of my works on *Colin Kaepernick, Aaron Rodgers, Peyton Manning, Tom Brady, Russell Wilson, Michael Jordan, LeBron James, Kyrie Irving, Klay Thompson, Anthony Davis, Stephen Curry, Kevin Durant, Russell Westbrook, Chris Paul, Kobe Bryant, Joakim Noah,*

Scottie Pippen, Carmelo Anthony, Kevin Love, Grant Hill, Tracy McGrady, Vince Carter, Patrick Ewing, Karl Malone, Tony Parker, Allen Iverson, Hakeem Olajuwon, Reggie Miller, Michael Carter-Williams, John Wall, James Harden, Tim Duncan, and *Steve Nash* in the Kindle Store. If you love basketball, check out my website at claytongeoffreys.com to join my exclusive list where I let you know about my latest books and give you lots of goodies.

Like what you read?

If you love books on life, basketball, or productivity, check out my website at claytongeoffreys.com to join my exclusive list where I let you know about my latest books. Aside from being the first to hear about my latest releases, you can also download a free copy of *33 Life Lessons: Success Principles, Career Advice & Habits of Successful People.* See you there!

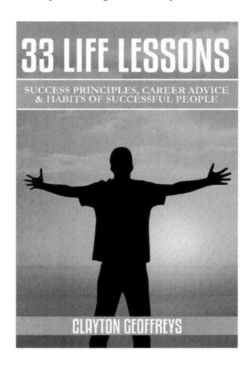

Made in the USA
San Bernardino, CA
21 December 2015